Wild Words from Wild Women

Other books in the Wild Women series

Wild Women
*Crusaders, Curmudgeons, and Completely Corsetless Ladies
in the Otherwise Virtuous Victorian Era*
by Autumn Stephens

Uppity Women of Ancient Times
by Vicki León

Wild Women in the Kitchen
101 Rambunctious Recipes and 99 Tasty Tales
by the Wild Woman Association
Introduction by Autumn Stephens

Wild Words from Wild Women

An Unbridled Collection of Candid Observations

&

Extremely Opinionated Bon Mots

collected by
Autumn Stephens

Conari Press · Berkeley, Calif.

Ϙ

CONARI PRESS

Conari Press books are distributed by Publishers Group West.

Cover design: Leigh Wells
Cover photograph: Archive Photos

ISBN: 1-57324-038-9

Library of Congress Cataloging-in-Publication Data
Stephens, Autumn, 1956–
[Untamed Tongues]
Wild words from wild women : an unbridled collection of candid observations
& extremely opinionated bon mots / Autumn Stephens.
p.   cm.
Includes index.
ISBN 1-57324-038-9 (paper)
1. Women—Quotations.   I. Title
PN6084.W6S74   1996
082'.082—dc20   95-46973

Printed in the United States of America on recycled paper.

10 9 8 7 6 5 4 3 2 1

Can We Talk?

Once we loved Barbie, the dishy doll with the missile-shaped bosoms and the pouty, slightly parted plastic lips. Unfortunately, little Miss Implant didn't have much to say for herself: She was too busy trying on all those cunning size 1/2 costumes (though I think she did occasionally emit a coy giggle when Ken tried to get cuddly).

Then came Chatty Cathy, flagrantly flat-chested and corporeally quite charmless—but oh, how that baby could babble! We pulled her string and pulled her string, until one sad day her motor-mouth simply sputtered and died, never again to blurt out those startling, solipsistic demands for juice or a journey to the zoo.

Finally, we fell for Madonna, a self-proclaimed boy-toy (though obviously she liked girls just fine too) who proved that you could have mam-mary glands *and* a jaw that opens all the way. "Listen," she said, "everyone is entitled to my opinion." And just in case we didn't think her smile was smug enough already, she wrapped it around a Coke bottle to prove her point.

This book is for Andrea's daughter, and Margaret's, and all the other little Madonna-ettes who will, I hope, grow up knowing how to do more with their breasts than beat them, and more with their mouths than paint them stop-sign red.

Garrulous Goddesses

$\mathcal{I}$'m tough, ambitious, and I know exactly what I want. If that makes me a bitch, okay.

$\mathcal{I}$ can throw a fit, I'm a master at it.

—MADONNA, chameleonesque queen of chutzpah.

$\mathcal{T}$he opposite of talking isn't listening. The opposite of talking is waiting.

$\mathcal{T}$he telephone is a good way to talk to people without having to offer them a drink.

$\mathcal{S}$uccess didn't spoil me; I've always been insufferable.

—Satirist FRAN LEBOWITZ, an inspiration to every sarcastic smart-ass who ever got herself booted out of high school.

$\mathcal{B}$esides Shakespeare and me, who do you think there is?

$\mathcal{I}$t takes a lot of time to be a genius, you have to sit around so much doing nothing, really doing nothing.

$\mathcal{T}$he Jews have produced only three originative geniuses: Christ, Spinoza, and myself.

—Writer GERTRUDE STEIN, who loomed large in the avant-garde circles of her day, and larger still in the privacy of her own mind.

*J*ust being in a room with myself is almost more stimulation than I can bear.

—KATE BRAVERMAN, agitated author of the cult classic *Lithium for Medea*.

I would live in a communist country providing I was the Queen.

—STELLA ADLER, Methodic mentor to big screen kings Marlon Brando, Warren Beatty and Robert De Niro. ("If she were a character in a Greek play," one interviewer concluded, "her flaw would be hubris.")

$\mathcal{I}$ have a horror of death; the dead are so soon forgotten. But when I die, they'll have to remember me.

—EMILY DICKINSON, a poet far too singular to slip anybody's mind.

$\mathcal{I}$ now know all the people worth knowing in America and I find no intellect comparable to my own.

—MARGARET FULLER. The brilliant Bostonian who wrote *Woman in the Nineteenth Century* was a shocking exhibitionist when it came to her brain.

$\mathcal{T}$he more articulate one is, the more dangerous words become.

—Prolific poet/prosaist MAY SARTON, a major menace to society.

I have a simple philosophy: Fill what's empty. Empty what's full. Scratch where it itches.

If you haven't got anything nice to say about anybody, come sit next to me.

—ALICE ROOSEVELT LONGWORTH, one of America's nastiest national institutions.

Show me someone who never gossips, and I'll show you someone who isn't interested in people.

   —Broadcast newswoman BARBARA WALTERS, a very caring conversationalist.

Learning to speak is like learning to shoot.

   —Professor AVITAL RONELL, comparative literature specialist, and a self-proclaimed "ivory-tower terrorist."

The people I'm furious with are the women's liberationists. They keep getting up on soap boxes and proclaiming that women are brighter than men. It's true, but it should be kept quiet or it ruins the whole racket.

—Screenwriter ANITA LOOS, who maintained that gentlemen were incapable of appreciating either brunettes or the basic facts of life.

$\mathcal{I}$ wasn't allowed to speak while my husband was alive, and since he's gone no one has been able to shut me up.

$\mathcal{N}$obody's interested in sweetness and light.

—God-like gossip columnist HEDDA HOPPER. With a flick of her poisonous pen, she could write a Hollywood hopeful right out of the picture.

I think if women would indulge more freely in vituperation, they would enjoy ten times the health they do. It seems to me they are suffering from repression.

*S*o long as women are slaves, men will be knaves.

—ELIZABETH CADY STANTON, the strapping spokeswoman for nineteenth-century suffragists.

$\mathcal{B}$e critical. Women have the right to say: This is surface, this falsifies reality, this degrades.

—TILLIE OLSEN. After twenty years of transcribing other people's words, the long-suppressed author of *Silences* finally found her own voice.

$\mathcal{W}$e are all born charming, fresh and spontaneous, and must be civilized before we are fit to participate in society.

—American etiquette maven MISS MANNERS, née JUDITH MARTIN, apparently not to the (excruciatingly correct) manner born.

$\mathcal{I}$ am terribly shy, but of course no one believes me. Come to think of it, neither would I.

    —CAROL CHANNING. Shy, perhaps, but scarcely retiring: in her eighth decade of life, *Hello Dolly* is still a happening thing.

I personally think we developed language because of our deep inner need to complain.

*R*eality is the leading cause of stress for those in touch with it.

*D*elusions of grandeur make me feel a lot better about myself.

—Writer JANE WAGNER, the wry collaborative mind behind some of Lily Tomlin's best lines.

Gossip is news running ahead of itself in a red satin dress.

—Syndicated columnist LIZ SMITH, dedicated to keeping a news-hungry nation apprised of the triumphs, tragedies, and predictable little peccadillos of those who live in (or for) the limelight.

A gossip is someone who talks to you about others, a bore is one who talks to you about himself, and a brilliant conversationalist is one who talks to you about yourself.

—Singer LISA KIRK, waxing eloquent on the subject of oral emissions.

$\mathcal{P}$eople call me feminist whenever I express sentiments that differentiate me from a doormat or a prostitute.

—Writer REBECCA WEST, puzzled (but not insulted) by the F-word.

$\mathcal{M}$y goal is to be accused of being strident.

—SUSAN FALUDI, scribe of the stinging *Backlash*.

Raving

Beauties

$\mathcal{I}$ don't have the time every day to put on makeup. I need that time to clean my rifle.

—HENRIETTE MANTEL, cosmetically incorrect comedian.

You'd be surprised how much it costs to look this cheap.

Lots of women buy just as many wigs and makeup things as I do. They just don't wear them all at the same time.

It's a good thing that I was born a woman, or I'd have been a drag queen.

   —DOLLY PARTON, rags-to-riches country music mogul. (In her dimestore days, desperate Dolly saved face by rouging her lips with Mercurochrome.)

*I*f you have formed the habit of checking on every new diet that comes along, you will find that, mercifully, they all blur together, leaving you with only one definite piece of information: french-fried potatoes are out.

I'm tired of all this nonsense about beauty being only skin-deep. That's deep enough. What do you want, an adorable pancreas?

   —JEAN KERR, perfectly attractive playwright whose modest goal was "to make a lot of people laugh and to make a lot of money."

$\mathcal{T}$aking joy in life is a woman's best cosmetic.

—ROSALIND RUSSELL, minimalist *Auntie Mame* who also suffered from the misconception that an appealing lunch could be fashioned solely from an assortment of cheeses.

$\mathcal{N}$ature has made women with a bosom, so nature thought it was important. Who am I to argue with nature?

—IDA ROSENTHAL, inventor of the modernbrassiere. She figured out how to gently lift and separate the women from the girls.

$\mathcal{M}$y husband said he wanted to have a relationship with a redhead, so I dyed my hair red.

—Activist/film star JANE FONDA, capable of changing her colors at the drop of an aerobics sock.

$\mathcal{I}$'ve never been lifted. But I do like a bit of glamour in the morning.

—Artist LOUISE NEVELSON. She preferred to be the sculptor, not the sculpture.

$\mathcal{A}$ny girl can be glamorous. All you have to do is stand still and look stupid.

—HEDY LAMARR. A much-coveted property pursuant to her elegantly unclad performance in the 1933 film *Ecstasy;* lovely Lamarr was smarter than she looked.

$\mathcal{I}$ dress for women, and undress for men.

—ANGIE DICKINSON. In or out of uniform, TV's leggy *Police Woman* inspired illicit fantasies.

$\mathcal{I}$t is possible that blondes also prefer gentlemen.

—MAMIE VAN DOREN, the *other* platinum bombshell of the fifties.

I have too many fantasies to be a housewife . . . I guess I *am* a fantasy.

I've been on a calendar, but never on time.

I am always running into people's unconscious.

I have never quite understood this sex symbol business, but if I'm going to be a symbol of something, I'd rather have it sex than some of the other things they've got symbols for.

—MARILYN MONROE, dead movie star. Was too much feminine mystique her fatal mistake?

$\mathcal{A}$ comparison between Madonna and me is a comparison between a strapless evening gown and a gownless evening strap.

—KIM CAMPBELL, erstwhile Prime Minister of Canada, criticized for emulating America's sexy boy-toy when she bared her forty-six-year-old shoulders in a pre-election photo.

$\mathcal{I}$ had to use ham. I took a piece from the deli platter and rubbed it in my hair. I had to—that fluffy thing was really bothering me.

—Alternative rock 'n roller KIM DEAL, on how to handle a bad hair day when you're way too cool for gel.

We're supposed to be attractive to the male to procreate the species, after all. That's why you've got to wear makeup and you've got to f***.

Women should try to increase their size rather than decrease it, because I believe the bigger we are, the more space we'll take up, and the more we'll have to be reckoned with. I think every woman should be fat like me.

People say to me, "You're not very feminine." Well, they can *suck my dick*.

—ROSEANNE, outsized sit-com star known both for her cheeky charm and for the cheeks themselves, revealed to an entire stadium of World Series fans during a 1989 mooning spree.

$\mathcal{A}$ diet counselor once told me that all overweight people are angry with their mothers and channel their frustrations into overeating. So I guess that means all thin people are happy, calm, and have resolved their Oedipal entanglements.

—WENDY WASSERSTEIN, perpetually plump ("I was an elementary school Falstaff") winner of the 1989 Pulitzer Prize for Drama.

There's nothing on earth to do here but look at the view and eat. You can imagine the result since I do not like to look at views.

—Famous wife ZELDA FITZGERALD, in a moment of Jazz Age angst. Flappers were supposed to be flat, not fleshy.

If American men are obsessed with money, American women are obsessed with weight. The men talk of gain, the women talk of loss, and I do not know which talk is the more boring.

—MARYA MANNES, journalist/OSS intelligence analyst. It didn't take her long to crack the nation's conversational code.

I never worry about diets. The only carrots that interest me are the number you get in a diamond.

*T*oo much of a good thing can be wonderful.

*W*hen women go wrong, men go right after them.

—Sex goddess MAE WEST, honored in 1933 by the Central Association of Obstetricians and Gynecologists for "popularizing the natural plumpness of the female figure."

$\mathcal{W}$hen women are depressed they either eat or go shopping. Men invade another country. It's a whole different way of thinking.

$\mathcal{I}$'m just a person trapped inside a woman's body.

—Comedian ELAYNE BOOSLER. Rejected by the Joffrey Ballet school for being non-bulimic, she became a substantial *Showtime* star by default.

$\mathcal{I}$ deliberately overeat to give my body the . . . most voluptuous contours I can acquire. Growing fatter is one of the most intensely sensuous things that I have ever experienced.

—MARGARET DEIRDRE O'HARTIGAN, sensuouswoman at large.

$\mathcal{A}$ woman is as young as her knees.

—British fashion designer MARY QUANT, revered by the leggy and reviled by the lumpy for creating, in the sexy Sixties, that very minimal method of covering the gluteus maximus still known as the mini-skirt.

$\mathcal{I}$ know there are some nights when I have power, when I could put on something and walk in somewhere, and if there is a man who doesn't look at me, it's because he's gay.

—Super-self-confident movie star KATHLEEN TURNER. If he doesn't leer, he must be queer. (Or could it be that his mama just raised him right?)

Scheherazade is easy; a little black dress is very difficult.

Elegance is refusal.

    —French couturier GABRIELLE "COCO" CHANEL, celebrated by modern young women of the 1920s for liberating them from the bonds of severely structured clothing, and by any number of modern young men as well, for succeeding where they had not.

$\mathcal{T}$here are no ugly women, only lazy ones.

  —HELENA RUBINSTEIN. Hard work made her a make-up magnate.

$\mathcal{I}$t's not what you'd call a figure, is it?

  —TWIGGY, Sixties supermodel famous for her lack of flesh. Spindly but not stupid, La Twig was hip to the fact that less is definitely more (to the fashion media's taste).

$\mathcal{M}$y weakness is wearing too much leopard print.

—Hollywood Novelist JACKIE COLLINS: often leonine; seldom lionized.

$\mathcal{I}$ base most of my fashion taste on what doesn't itch.

—Comedian GILDA RADNER. Fortunately, sensitive-skinned Gilda wound up as a *Saturday Night Live* star and not, like so many other unfortunate females of the polyester-and-pantyhose generation, as a resident of a nudist colony.

$\mathcal{I}$ did not have three thousand pairs of shoes, I had one thousand and sixty.

—IMELDA MARCOS, former First Lady of the Philippines, setting the record straight on her vast (but not quite so vast as previously assumed) collection of stilettos, slippers, scuffs, moccasins, mules, platforms, pumps, loafers, loungers, booties, button-ups, espadrilles, high heels, Mary Janes, tennies, golf shoes, and riding boots.

$\mathcal{A}$nyone with more than 365 pairs of shoes is a pig.

—BARBARA MELSER LIEBERMAN, setting the record straight on Imelda Marcos.

*I*t matters more what's in a woman's face than what's on it.

    —CLAUDETTE COLBERT, one actress who didn't lose any sleep over her lines.

*S*o many women just don't know how great they really are. They come to us all vogue outside and vague on the inside.

    —MARY KAY ASH, founder of the fantastically successful Mary Kay Cosmetics, Inc. Ironically, Ash proved her own mettle by selling lots of . . . make-up.

$\mathcal{I}$ never go out unless I look like Joan Crawford the movie star. If you want to see the girl next door, go next door.

—Actress JOAN CRAWFORD. For her fans, Mommie Dearest put her best face forward.

*Y*ou don't have to signal a social conscience by looking like a frump. Lace knickers won't hasten the holocaust, you can ban the bomb in a feather boa just as well without, and a mild interest in hemlines doesn't necessarily disqualify you from reading *Das Kapital* and agreeing with every word.

—British journalist JILL TWEEDIE. Oh, go ahead and smash the state if you must—but just this once, it wouldn't kill you to put on a little make-up!

What is beautiful is good,
And who is good will soon be beautiful.

 —SAPPHO, gal-loving Greek poet. And who is *neither* beautiful nor good, it seems, is just plain out of the loop.

Never darken my Dior again!

 —British actress BEATRICE LILLIE, displaying great Christian charity toward the waiter who accidentally dumped dinner onto her dress.

*W*hat you eat standing up doesn't count.

    —Creative calorie-counter BETH BARNES, the right-brained dieter's answer to Richard Simmons.

*K*iss my shapely big fat ass.

    —Country crooner K.T. OSLIN, whose much-publicized menopause made her a trifle less petite, and far more impolite.

Political Animas
&
Public Enemies

I want to be more than a rose in my husband's lapel.

I want two passports. I want a passport that says "wife of the Prime Minister" and a passport that says I'm free.

    —MARGARET TRUDEAU, a sexy side-kick in the pants to her Studio 54 pals; a mondo thorn in the side for poor Pierre.

Remember the Ladies, and be more generous and favorable to them than your ancestors. Do not put such unlimited power into the hands of the Husbands. Remember all Men would be tyrants if they could. If particular care and attention is not paid to the Ladies we are determined to foment a Rebellion, and will not hold ourselves bound by any Laws in which we have no voice, or Representation.

—ABIGAIL ADAMS, wife of the second president of the United States of America.

*S*ometimes when I look at my children I say to myself, "Lillian, you should have stayed a virgin."

—LILLIAN CARTER, mother of the thirty-ninth president of the United States of America.

*W*ell, I've got you the presidency, what are you going to do with it?

—FLORENCE HARDING, wife of the twenty-ninth president of the United States of America.

$\mathcal{E}$very politician should have been born an orphan and remain a bachelor.

—LADY BIRD JOHNSON, wife of the thirty-sixth president of the United States of America.

$\mathcal{B}$ehind every successful man is a surprised woman.

—MARYON PEARSON, former Canadian Prime Minister's wife.

$\mathcal{T}$he position of First Lady has no rules, just precedent, so its evolution has been at a virtual standstill for years. If Martha Washington didn't do it, then no one is sure it should be done.

—PAULA POUNDSTONE, social satirist with no political or marital ambitions whatsoever.

$\mathcal{I}$ suppose I could have stayed home and baked cookies and had teas.

—HILLARY CLINTON, wife of the forty-second president of the United States of America.

One cannot be too extreme in dealing with social ills; besides, the extreme thing is generally the true thing.

There's never been a good government.

—EMMA GOLDMAN. Often arrested for anarchy, "Red Emma" had plenty of solitary time to contemplate the numerous sins of the state.

If American politics are too dirty for women to take part in, there's something wrong with American politics.

—Writer EDNA FERBER, an ornery "old maid" who called them like she saw them.

There is little place in the political scheme of things for an independent, creative personality, for a fighter. Anyone who takes that role must pay a price.

—SHIRLEY CHISHOLM, professor and practitioner of political science, and the first black woman to battle her way into Congress.

$\mathcal{I}$'m no lady; I'm a member of Congress, and I'll proceed on that basis.

—MARY NORTON, the first Democrat with breasts ever elected to Congress entirely on her own merits, rather than creeping in on the coattails of a deceased spouse.

$\mathcal{I}$ have a brain and a uterus, and I use both.

$\mathcal{W}$hen people ask me why I am running as a woman, I always answer, "What choice do I have?"

—PATRICIA SCHROEDER, veteran Colorado congresswoman who coined the term "Teflon-coated presidency," also known as Mom.

$\mathcal{T}$he test for whether or not you can hold a job should not be the arrangement of your chromosomes.

$\mathcal{O}$ur struggle today is not to have a female Einstein get appointed as an assistant professor. It is for a woman schlemiel to get as quickly promoted as a male schlemiel.

$\mathcal{I}$'m no Joanna come lately, believe me, I've been here all along—outside. (Upon being elected to U.S. House of Representatives in 1971.)

$\mathcal{A}$ll the men on my staff can type.

—BELLA ABZUG, three-term U.S. Congresswoman from New York, known both for the unconventional contents of her cranium and her penchant for placing ladylike *chapeaux* on it.

$\mathcal{D}$r. Kissinger was surprised that I knew where Ghana was.

—SHIRLEY TEMPLE BLACK, former Ambassador to Ghana. ("The Good Ship Lollipop," all-grown-up Shirley once noted diplomatically, "is now in drydock.")

$\mathcal{W}$inning may not be everything, but losing has little to recommend it.

—SENATOR DIANNE FEINSTEIN, the only powerhouse politico to dress for success in blouses with built-in bows.

You can no more win a war than you can win an earthquake.

As a woman I can't go to war, and I refuse to send anyone else.

—JEANETTE RANKIN, first woman to serve in Congress, and the sole member of either house to vote against U.S. entry into World War II.

*M*an has been given his freedom to a greater extent than ever and that's quite wrong.

*E*verybody should rise up and say, "Thank you, Mr. President, for bombing Haiphong."

—Infamous Watergate wife MARTHA MITCHELL, who demonstrated the inherent nonviolent nature of womankind.

$\mathcal{I}$ wouldn't be satisfied with a life lived solely on the barricades. I reserve my right to be frivolous.

—Frolicsome BETTY FRIEDAN, the mother of modern American feminism.

I don't notice that I'm a woman. I regard myself as the Prime Minister.

*I*n politics, if you want anything said, ask a man; if you want anything done, ask a woman.

*O*ne of the things that politics has taught me is that men are not a reasoned or reasonable sex.

—MARGARET THATCHER. The "Iron Lady" who served as the United Kingdom's first female Prime Minister was capable of almost anything—including, on occasion, irony.

$\mathcal{W}$ar is menstrual envy!

—Feminist anti-war slogan. (So what's the cure—radical histerectomy?)

$\mathcal{A}$ woman is like a teabag—you can't tell how strong she is until you put her in hot water.

—The astrologically aware NANCY REAGAN, an old hand at the heated H_2O experience.

$\mathcal{I}$ would not have gotten [to Congress] if I had not been more persistent than a hound dog worrying a bone.

—Idaho Congresswoman GRACIE PFOST. Note: In most sexist states, an ambitious woman must not only worry the bone, but actually cause it to have a nervous breakdown.

Under conditions of tyranny it is far easier to act than to think.

It is well known that the most radical revolutionary will become a conservative on the day after the revolution.

—HANNAH ARENDT, left-wing philosopher who promoted the radical notion that morality might have a place in politics.

*I*f [women] understood and exercised their power they could remake the world.

    —Illinois congresswoman EMILY TAFT DOUGLAS, not the first woman in the world to suggest that the original Creator didn't come up with the most user-friendly model.

I've always argued that it is just as desirable, just as possible, to have philosopher plumbers as philosopher kings.

    —EDITH STARRETT GREEN, Oregon congresswoman.
Either way, we suppose, a lot of bullshit is inevitable.

There's one sure way of telling when politicians aren't telling the truth—their lips move.

—British actress FELICITY KENDALL, on the subject of professional prevaricators.

It is not lack of polling data or campaign contributions which keeps many women from ascending higher on the political ladder. It is fear and loathing for the political system itself.

—Governor MADELEINE KUNIN of Vermont, one woman who didn't run in fear.

*Y*ou can fool all of the people some of the time, and some of the people all of the time. And that's sufficient.

—ROSE KING, a rather realistic political consultant.

*Y*ears ago, fairy tales all began with "Once upon a time . . ."—now we know they all begin with, "If I am elected."

—CAROLYN WARNER, 1986 Democratic nominee for governor of Arizona. (Worse yet, they so seldom end with "And they all lived happily ever after.")

$\mathcal{T}$he mistake a lot of politicians make is in forgetting they've been appointed and thinking they've been anointed.

—Florida politics-follower MRS. CLAUDE PEPPER, no friend of the overtly oily.

$\mathcal{Y}$ou can't shake hands with a clenched fist.

—INDIRA GANDHI. Ironically, India's prominent female Prime Minister perished at the hands of assassins.

$\mathcal{W}$ar is not nice.

—Former First Lady BARBARA BUSH. Like many less famous spouses, she shared her husband's house—but not always his point of view.

$\mathcal{I}$'d like to see a women's army storm into the White House with Uzis and shotguns and eliminate at least half the population whowork in politics. They're killing you slowly—what's the alternative? Kill them quickly, kill them now—before they kill everything else, okay?

—LYDIA LUNCH, former vocalist for "Teenage Jesus and the Jerks," no longer sublimating her rage.

Libidinous Lingo

&

Tart Retorts

*A*ll that you suspect about women's friendships is true. We talk about dick size.

    —CYNTHIA HEIMEL, well-informed author of *Sex Tips for Girls*, and evidently an excellent conversationalist as well.

*W*omen's virtue is man's greatest invention.

    —CORNELIA OTIS SKINNER, author, actress, and the narrator of an informative NBC broadcast about debutantes in the sixties.

$\mathcal{T}$he nicest women in our "society" are raving sex maniacs. But, being just awfully, awfully nice they don't, of course, descend to fucking—that's uncouth—rather they make love, commune by means of their bodies and establish sensual rapport.

. . . $\mathcal{T}$he male function is to produce sperm. We now have sperm banks.

—VALERIE SOLANIS, who furthered the feminist cause by founding SCUM (Society for Cutting Up Men) and attempting to assassinate Andy Warhol.

$\mathcal{T}$here are two kinds of women: those who want power in the world, and those who want power in bed.

    —JACQUELINE KENNEDY ONASSIS, supremely successful serial monogamist.

$\mathcal{I}$'m not saying that I'd vote for him. I'm just saying that I'd fuck him.

    —Actress MAUREEN STAPLETON, always liberal with her love, on the subject of her strange attraction for George Bush.

$\mathcal{I}$ wish I had as much in bed as I get in the newspapers.

—LINDA RONSTADT, prolific pop singer who posed the poignant musical question: *When Will I Be Loved?*

$\mathcal{R}$ock is really about dick and testosterone. I go see a band, I wanna fuck the guy—that's the way it is; it's always been that way.

—COURTNEY LOVE, paradoxically phallocentric (well, on occasion, anyway) founder of the rock band "Hole."

$\mathcal{A}$ healthy sex life. Best thing in the world for a woman's voice.

    —LEONTYNE PRICE, world-renowned soprano.

$\mathcal{T}$he prerequisite for making love is to like someone enormously.

    —Magazine editor HELEN GURLEY BROWN. Yes, even those cleavage-baring *Cosmo* girls draw the line *somewhere!*

$\mathcal{I}$ am a free lover!

—VICTORIA WOODHULL, the very unmarried candidate for U.S. presidency in 1872, clarifying her official position on domestic relations.

$\mathcal{A}$ mutual and satisfied sexual act is of great benefit to the average woman, the magnetism of it is health giving. When it is not desired on the part of the woman and she has no response, *it should not take place*. This is an act of prostitution and is degrading to the woman's finer sensibility, all the marriage certificates on earth to the contrary notwithstanding.

—Birth control pioneer MARGARET SANGER, 1917. All in all, she was jailed nine times for her belief that offspring were optional.

My reaction to porno films is as follows: After the first ten minutes, I want to go home and screw. After the first twenty minutes, I never want to screw again as long as I live.

—ERICA JONG, author of *Fear of Flying* (the seminal sexual liberation novel of the 1970s), once characterized by a fellow writer as "a mammoth pudenda."

I've tried several varieties of sex. The conventional position makes me claustrophobic. And the others either give me a stiff neck or lockjaw.

—TALLULAH BANKHEAD. Even after considerable erotic experimentation, the agile actress remained (so she claimed) "as pure as the driven slush."

*U*ntil you've lost your reputation, you never realize what a burden it was or what freedom really is.

    —Epic novelist MARGARET MITCHELL. Evidently the antebellum South wasn't the only thing that was *Gone With the Wind*.

*I*n my sex fantasy, nobody ever loves me for my mind.

    —Sizzling screenwriter NORA EPHRON, actually (or so one interviewer assures us) "much prettier than she appears in most of her pictures."

$\mathcal{M}$y own, or other people's?

—PEGGY GUGGENHEIM, exceedingly amorous art patron, in response to the question "How many husbands have you had?"

A different kind of dame gets a different kind of fame.

*A*s far as I'm concerned, morality is just a word that describes the current fashion of conduct.

*I*t seems to me that basically a woman who sells her emotions in bed, often pretending love and affection, is as great an actress as one who sells her beauty and emotions to the camera or the public. Personally, I trust most prostitutes further than the actresses I've known.

—SALLY STANFORD, self-made madam and vice-mayor of Sausalito, California

$\mathcal{I}$ never made any money till I took off my pants.

—Exotic dancer SALLY RAND, famous for her well-placed fans.

$\mathcal{I}$ ran the wrong kind of business, but I did it with integrity.

—SIDNEY BIDDLE BARROWS, the so-called "Mayflower Madam." Just as they say, breeding *does* indeed tell . . .

*T*he world wants to be cheated. So cheat.

*S*omething is wrong here: sex has been with us since the human race began its existence, yet I would estimate that 90 percent of human beings still suffer from enormous inhibitions in this area.

—XAVIERA HOLLANDER, a.k.a. *The Happy Hooker*. Her bawdy Pill-era bestsellers provided millions of junior-high virgins with useful information about mate-swapping, sex with other species, and amusing stunts to perform on public escalators.

The real fountain of youth is to have a dirty mind.

My mother said it was simple to keep a man; you must be a maid in the living room, a cook in the kitchen and a whore in the bedroom. I said I'd hire the other two and take care of the bedroom bit.

Even if you only have two seconds drop everything and give him a blow job. That way he won't really want sex with anyone else.

—JERRY HALL, former Texan model and vice versa, sharing her strategy for encouraging mate Mick Jagger to spend some quality time at home.

$\mathcal{U}$nless there's some emotional tie, I'd rather play tennis.

—BIANCA JAGGER, former jet-setting Beautiful Person and Rolling Stone spouse. Hence, perhaps, the Stone's raunchy rock anthem *(I Can't Get No) Satisfaction*?

$\mathcal{W}$hen one is pretending, the entire body revolts.

—ANAÏS NIN. Not as candid as she claimed, naughty Nin inflated her notorious Diaries with accounts of imaginary affairs, and edited other lovers right out of literary history.

$\mathcal{Y}$ou mustn't force sex to do the work of love or love to do the work of sex.

—Prolific prose-writer MARY McCARTHY, who got a lot of grief for focusing on "feminine gossip" in *The Group,* her noteworthy 1963 novel about female college graduates.

$\mathcal{R}$eally that little dealybob is too far away from the hole. It should be built right in.

—Country singer LORETTA LYNN, not afraid to get literal about the clitoral.

*I*f I had a cock for a day, I would get myself pregnant.

—GERMAINE GREER, Australia's foremost feminist. Somehow, renting just isn't the same as owning.

I'm saving the bass player for Omaha.

—Rock icon JANIS JOPLIN, in a rare moment of self-restraint.

*I*t doesn't matter what you do in the bedroom as long as you don't do it in the street and frighten the horses.

    —British actress MRS. PATRICK CAMPBELL. At the turn of the century, safe sex was much, much simpler.

I am happy now that Charles calls on my bed chamber less frequently than of old. As it is I now endure but two calls a week and when I hear his steps outside my door I lie down on my bed, close my eyes, open my legs and think of England.

    —LADY ALICE HILLINGDON, who never, ever frightened a horse in her life.

*J*ust close your eyes, think of England, and collect your money.

—Anonymous female movie studio executive on the subject of Hollywood Madam HEIDI FLEISS. From the financial perspective, sex without passion is seldom pointless.

$\mathcal{T}$he average man is more interested in a woman who is interested in him than he is in a woman—any woman—with beautiful legs.

$\mathcal{I}$n America sex is an obsession, in other parts of the world it is a fact.

—MARLENE DIETRICH. The exotic star of *The Blue Angel* and *Blonde Venus* didn't get all worked up about nothing.

$\mathcal{A}$ kiss is a lovely trick designed by nature to stop speech when words become superfluous.

$\mathcal{H}$appiness is good health and a bad memory.

—Actress INGRID BERGMAN, whose adulterous pre-marital affair with film director Robert Rossellini set tongues wagging around the world.

$\mathcal{W}$hatever else can be said about sex, it cannot be called a dignified performance.

—Writer HELEN LAWRENSON. But then again, who's watching?

$\mathcal{S}$ex is the tabasco sauce which an adolescent national palate sprinkles on every course in the menu.

—Writer MARY DAY WINN. The American approach to amour made her lose her appetite.

Coition, sometimes called "the little death," is more like a slight attack of apoplexy.

—PAULINE SHAPLER. In the end, love is so seldom a pretty thing.

A man on a date wonders if he'll get lucky. The woman already knows.

—Prescient MONICA PIPER. The suspense isn't killing her.

*W*hy do I show my cervix? I tell the audience that the reason I show my cervix is: 1) because it's fun—and I think fun is really important, and 2) because the cervix is so beautiful that I really want to share that with people.

—ANNIE SPRINKLE, former sex film star who now prefers to package her wholesome public exhibitions as performance art.

Out & About

*O*ne thing I've noticed in particular about straight people—and I've known a lot of them so I think I can talk—is that when they find out you're lesbian, they inevitably ask, sooner or later, this famous question: "Why is it that so *many* lesbians dress like men?"

—KATE GAWF, artist/writer who refrains from crass speculation on the relationship between sexual and sartorial orientation. *She,* for one, does not "sit around wondering whether the Pope has a boyfriend."

Once you know what women are like, men get kind of boring. I'm not trying to put them down, I mean I like them sometimes as people, but sexually they're dull.

A life of reaction is a life of slavery, intellectually and spiritually. One must fight for a life of action, not reaction.

Lead me not into temptation; I can find the way myself.

—RITA MAE BROWN. Enough said. "Next time anybody calls me a lesbian writer," Ms. Brown once remarked, "I'm going to knock their teeth in."

$\mathcal{I}$ was eight years old and she [Eleanor Roosevelt] came to the Easter Egg Roll wearing jodhpurs and riding boots. I'm *sure* that had an influence on my life . . .

—SALLY GEARHART, graphic sapphic, speculating wildly on the origins of her sexual preference.

$\mathcal{I}$f you have one gay experience, does that mean you're gay? If you have one heterosexual experience, does that mean you're straight? Life doesn't work quite so cut and dried.

—BILLIE JEAN KING, tennis champion who put a new spin on the phrase *love-all* when she copped to an extra-marital lesbian love affair. ("It's not contagious," Billie's highly evolved husband assured the press. "I didn't catch it.")

$\mathcal{I}$n the heterosexual imagination, everything that gay people do becomes sexualized. They think that's all we're doing, and unfortunately, it's not. I wish that being a lesbian were as juicy as I think Jesse Helms thinks it is.

—HOLLY HUGHES, obscenely unfunded performance artist who managed to steal a moment from her rigorous romantic schedule to sue the National Endowment for the Arts.

$\mathcal{I}$f you march around screaming "I'm a lesbian!" what good is it? I admire gay activists, but I'm an artist.

—K.D. LANG, Canadian-born chanteuse, vegetarian, teetotaler and animal rights activist who in 1993 apparently decided that coming out was better than acting out.

$\mathcal{L}$esbians are "dykes," not "dikes." We are not dams, although some people consider us damned.

—MARGARET A. ROBINSON, sensitive speller, in a candid 1973 letter to *Ms.* about her alphabetical (and other) preferences.

$\mathcal{I}$'m everything you were afraid your little girl would grow up to be—and your little boy.

—BETTE MIDLER. The "Divine Miss M." launched her multi-faceted entertainment career in gay bath-houses.

$\mathcal{W}$hat is most beautiful in virile men is something feminine; what is most beautiful in feminine women is something masculine.

—SUSAN SONTAG, seductive intellectual once touted as the "Natalie Wood of the U.S. Avant-Garde."

The word [androgyny] is misbegotten—conveying something like "John Travolta and Farrah Fawcett-Majors scotch-taped together."

—MARY DALY, the thinking woman's theologian.

Coming from Nazi Germany and having survived Hitler and the concentration camps, I am very worried when I hear the word quarantine. Because the next thing they might decide is everyone 4'7" should be quarantined.

—DR. RUTH WESTHEIMER, extra-small sex therapist, waxing wrathful over a proposal to segregate homosexuals and AIDS patients from the population at large.

*M*en have always been afraid that women could get along without them.

I think extreme heterosexuality is a perversion.

—MARGARET MEAD, world-famous anthropologist who, having devoted her life to studying the ways of all flesh, was certainly in a position to know.

*W*hy are women so much more interesting to men than men are to women?

*I*t is fatal for anyone who writes to think of their sex. It is fatal to be a man or woman pure and simple; one must be woman-manly or man-womanly.

> —Writer VIRGINIA WOOLF. For most members of the avant-garde Bloomsbury Circle, androgyny was where it was at.

*I*f anyone told *me* they were a "lesbian sex guru," I would tell them to get a life.

—Writer SUSIE BRIGHT, adamant that (all evidence to the contrary) her first name is definitely not "Lesbian sex guru."

*A*s far as I'm concerned, being any gender at all is a drag.

—Rock singer PATTI SMITH, who spent (perhaps not coincidentally) much of her youth reading Rimbaud and rapping with Robert Mapplethorpe.

Vocal
Oracles

$\mathcal{Y}$ou don't have to be dowdy to be a Christian.

—TAMMY FAYE BAKKER, ultra-lash evangelist. (Thou shalt not, however, skimp on eye shadow.)

$\mathcal{I}$f I were going to convert to any religion I would probably choose Catholicism because it at least has female saints and the Virgin Mary.

—MARGARET ATWOOD, Canada's pre-eminent pagan novelist, poet, and "high priestess of angst."

I learned that women were smart and capable, could live in community together without men, and in fact did not need men much.

—ANNA QUINDLEN, nun-educated essayist, on the feminist fringe benefits of attending parochial school.

*T*he only sin is mediocrity.

—MARTHA GRAHAM, patron saint of modern dance.

No good deed goes unpunished.

But if God had wanted us to think just with our wombs, why did He give us a brain?

—CLARE BOOTH LUCE, distinguished diplomat and a devout Catholic. (Before visiting the Vatican, Madam Ambassador had to swear to the Senate that she understood all about the separation of church and state.)

The cross is the symbol of torture; I prefer the dollar sign, the symbol of free trade, therefore of a free mind.

Every major horror of history was committed in the name of an altruistic motive. Has any act of selfishness ever equalled the carnage perpetrated by disciples of altruism?

—Rabid "radical capitalist" AYN RAND, who found the United States infinitely more congenial than post-revolutionary Russia.

*M*any are saved from sin by being so inept at it.

*O*ur strength is often composed of the weakness we're damned if we're going to show.

*M*ost sermons sound to me like commercials—but I can't make out whether God is the Sponsor or the Product.

    —MIGNON MCLAUGHLIN, self-confessed "neurotic." (Could channel-surfing be the cure?)

$\mathcal{I}$ felt it better to speak to God than about Him.

—ST. THERESE OF LISIEUX, not the type to talk behind the Supreme Being's back.

$\mathcal{F}$rom somber, serious, sullen saints, deliver us, O Lord, hear our prayer.

—ST. TERESA OF AVILA. Renowned for her quasi-orgasmic raptures, sexy Sister T. made faith look like a lot of fun.

There will be less external discipline the more internal discipline there is.

I can, therefore I am.

—Philosopher SIMONE WEIL, who chose to conduct a life of the mind in a state of poverty.

*N*o, I wouldn't touch a leper for a thousand pounds, yet I willingly cure him for the love of God.

*T*here should be less talk. A preaching point is not a meeting point.

—MOTHER TERESA, the modern world's most noted nun.

Somewhere, and I can't find where, I read about an Eskimo hunter who asked the local missionary priest, "If I did not know about God and sin, would I go to hell?" "No," said the priest, "not if you did not know." "Then why," asked the Eskimo earnestly, "did you tell me?"

 —Author ANNIE DILLARD in *Pilgrim at Tinker Creek*. When it comes to Christianity, a little knowledge is always a dangerous thing.

Good for the soul—but bad for the heel.

 —AGNES GUILFOYLE, no longer confused about the concept of confession.

$\mathcal{D}$id not God
Sometimes withhold in mercy what we ask,
We should be ruined at our own request.

$\mathcal{G}$enius, without religion, is only a lamp on the outer gate of a palace; it may serve to cast a gleam of light on those that are without, while the inhabitant is in darkness.

—Seventeenth-century poet HANNAH MORE, once accused of plagiarism, but never of withholding her theological views from the masses.

I always find that statistics are hard to swallow and impossible to digest. The only one I can ever remember is that if all the people who go to sleep in church were laid end to end they would be a lot more comfortable.

—MRS. ROBERT A. TAFT, spouse of an Ohio senator, on the demographics of dozing in pews.

*M*illions long for immortality who do not know what to do with themselves on a rainy Sunday afternoon.

—SUSAN ERTZ, novelist. If you can't handle a little ennui, eternity's not for you.

To eat bread without hope is still slowly to starve to death.

I feel no need for any other faith than my faith in human beings.

It may be that religion is dead, and if it is, we had better know it and set ourselves to try to discover other sources of moral strength before it is too late.

—PEARL S. BUCK. Her goal as a novelist was not only to entertain, but to enlighten.

Of course, there's no such thing as a totally objective person, except Almighty God, if she exists.

—Historian ANTONIA FRASER. (And if she does exist, boy, is she pissed off.)

I know God is not a woman—no woman would have created men with so many imperfections.

—JILL M. CONSIDEINE, who has faith that He is not a She.

*I*t is impossible to repent of love. The sin of love does not exist.

—MURIEL SPARK. The author of *The Prime of Miss Jean Brodie* converted to Catholicism, but refused to censor her heart.

*W*omen give themselves to God when the devil wants nothing more to do with them.

—Eighteenth-century opera singer SOPHIE ARNOULD. Whether the adulterous affair that destroyed her brilliant career was worth it in the end, God only knows.

$\mathcal{E}$vil dwells in moist places.

    —SISTER MARY OLIVIA, whose candid caveat speaks to every woman who has ever inadvertently hosted a yeast infection.

Conjugal Confessions
&
Solitary Digressions

$\mathcal{L}$et's face it, when an attractive but ALOOF ("cool") man comes along, there are some of us who offer to shine his shoes with our underpants.

—Cartoonist LYNDA BARRY, who completely understands that few women have anything in common with Sharon Stone.

She was always pleased to have him come and never sorry to see him go.

It [having an abortion] serves me right for putting all my eggs in one bastard.

I require only three things of a man. He must be handsome, ruthless and stupid.

—DOROTHY PARKER, whose minimal entrance requirements weren't precisely rigid. ("One more drink," the mistress of *mals mots* once confessed, "and I'd have been under the host.")

I never liked the men I loved, and I never loved the men I liked.

—FANNY BRICE. The leading lady of Ziegfeld's Follies had a few foibles (including a massive passion for a gangster) of her own.

$\mathcal{A}$ girl can wait for the right man to come along, but in the meantime that still doesn't mean she can't have a wonderful time with all the wrong ones.

$\mathcal{T}$he trouble with some women is that they get all excited about nothing—and then marry him.

$\mathcal{T}$he square people think I'm too hip and the hip people think I'm too square. And nobody likes my choice of men—everybody thinks I'm fucking the Mormon Tabernacle Choir.

   —CHER, perennially popular entertainer. (After all, *somebody's* got to date the youth of America.)

$\mathcal{W}$hen he's late for dinner, I know he's either having an affair or is lying dead in the street. I always hope it's the street.

—JESSICA TANDY, married to fellow actor Hume Cronyn for nearly one-half century, on the subject of driving Miss Daisy completely bonkers.

$\mathscr{I}$ have yet to hear a man ask for advice on how to combine marriage and a career.

$\mathscr{I}$ can't mate in captivity.

$\mathscr{S}$ome of us are becoming the men we wanted to marry.

—GLORIA STEINEM, the mother of all *Ms's*.

$\mathcal{T}$o be killed or to be married is the universal female fate.

—Nineteenth-century author ADELE M. FIELDE. In the deceptively decorous Victorian era, it was *fatale* not to be ultra-femme.

A woman need know but one man well, in order to understand all men; whereas a man may know all women and understand not one of them.

*B*efore a marriage, a man will lie awake all night thinking about something you said; after marriage, he'll fall asleep before you finish saying it.

A husband is what is left of the lover after the nerve is extracted.

*W*hen you see what some girls marry, you realize how they must hate to work for a living.

—Author HELEN ROWLAND. The woman who wrote *Reflections of a Bachelor Girl* had no aversion to applying herself.

$\mathcal{A}$ny intelligent woman who reads the marriage contract, and then goes into it, deserves all the consequences.

—ISADORA DUNCAN, the flamboyant foremother of contemporary dance. Impulsive Isadora enjoyed many lovers, but her sole spouse committed suicide after two short years of matrimony.

$\mathcal{I}$ have no wish for a second husband. I had enough of the first. I like to have my own way—to lie down mistress, and get up master.

—Canadian pioneer SUSANNA MOODIE. As a widow, she never got up on the wrong side of bed.

*B*eing alone and liking it is, for a woman, an act of treachery, an infidelity far more threatening than adultery.

> —Film critic MOLLY HASKELL, who reviewed several scenes from a marriage (hers, not Bergman's) and concluded that romantic love was essentially an "infectious disease."

*O*ne of the advantages of living alone is that you don't have to wake up in the arms of a loved one.

> —MARION SMITH, who prefers to rest in peace.

I don't need a man to rectify my existence. The most profound relationship we'll ever have is the one with ourselves.

—SHIRLEY MACLAINE, frequently reincarnated actress who, over the centuries, has already had more than her fair share of fellows anyway.

The world is my husband.

—ELSA MAXWELL, celebrated *bon vivant* who thought it perfectly possible to eat, drink and be unmarried.

$\mathcal{W}$hat a commentary on our civilization, when being alone is considered suspect; when one has to apologize for it, make excuses, hide the fact that one practices it—like a secret vice!

—Aviator/writer ANNE MORROW LINDBERGH. Happily wed to charming Charles, she envied nothing so much as the "austere peace" of monks.

Plain women know more about men than beautiful ones do.

Sometimes I wonder if men and women really suit each other. Perhaps they should live next door and just visit now and then.

—Actress KATHARINE HEPBURN, who got along famously with married lover Spencer Tracy during a quarter-century of now-and-then visits.

$\mathcal{A}$ll along, one of my major complaints was his absence from home, and even worse, his absence when he **was** home.

—SONIA JOHNSON, heretical housewife. Absence did not make her heart grow fonder.

$\mathcal{I}$ married beneath me. All women do.

—LADY NANCY ASTOR. Frankly, Britain's first female MP preferred the pedestal.

I would rather be a beggar and single, than a Queen and married. . . . I should call the wedding ring the yoke ring.

—QUEEN ELIZABETH I of England. An unmarried state of affairs suited Bess best.

*I*f a woman hasn't met the right man by the time she's 24, she may be lucky.

—Actress DEBORAH KERR. Appropriately enough, dubious Deborah's role in the movie *Dream Wife* was entirely comedic.

I never married because there was no need. I have three pets at home which answer the same purpose as a husband. I have a dog which growls every morning, a parrot which swears all afternoon and a cat that comes home late at night.

—MARIE CORELLI. Why settle for a man when you can have a menagerie à trois?

Nuns and married women are equally unhappy, if in different ways.

—QUEEN CHRISTINA of Sweden. Any way you looked at it in the 1600s, the Master was always a man, and vice versa.

$\mathcal{A}$ man is an accessory, like a pair of earrings. It may finish the outfit, but you don't really need it to keep you warm.

—ROSEMARY MITTLEMARK, equally unlikely to commit a crime of passion or one of fashion.

$\mathcal{T}$here is probably nothing like living together for blinding people to each other.

—IVY COMPTON-BURNETT, a novelist with 20/20 vision.

I think every woman is entitled to a middle husband she can forget.

*A*fter all, God made man and then said: I can do better than that —and made woman.

*T*here is so little difference between husbands you might as well keep the first.

  —ADELE ROGERS ST. JOHNS, who should probably take the Fifth on her true feelings about fellows.

For though I know he loves me
Tonight my heart is sad
His kiss was not so wonderful
As all the dreams I had.

No one worth possessing
Can be quite possessed.

—Pulitzer Prize-winning poet SARA TEASDALE, a soul almost (but not quite) too sensitive for words.

The poor wish to be rich, the rich wish to be happy, the single wish to be married, and the married wish to be dead.

—Advice columnist ANN LANDERS, an expert on what exasperates America.

*L*ove has been in perpetual strife with monogamy.

A great poet has seldom sung of lawfully wedded happiness, but often of free and secret love; and in this respect, too, the time is coming when there will no longer be one standard of morality for poetry, and another for life.

    —Nineteenth-century social reformer ELLEN KEY, free with her favors long before Swedish women were supposed to be sexually liberated.

The two sexes mutually corrupt and improve each other.

—MARY WOLLSTONECRAFT. In her *Vindication of the Rights of Women,* the literary libertine of eighteenth-century England told Jean Jacques Rousseau where he and his ideas about feminine inferiority could go.

Now at least I know where he is.

—QUEEN ALEXANDRA of Great Britain, contemplating her incipient widowhood. (Dead husbands don't fool around.)

*N*agging is the repetition of unpalatable truths.

—BARONESS EDITH SUMMERSKILL. The peerless peeress was President of Britain's Married Women's Association in the 1950s.

*M*y husband will never chase another woman. He's too fine, too decent, too old.

—Comedian GRACIE ALLEN. Having made the great George Burns "a success after years and years of failure," good-humored Gracie was also allowed to make a joke or two at his expense.

$\mathcal{E}$rrol Flynn died on a 70-foot boat with a 17-year-old girl. Walter has always wanted to go that way, but he's going to settle for a 17-footer with a 70-year-old.

—BETSY CRONKITE, wife of the firmly anchored Walter.

Almost all married people fight, although many are ashamed to admit it. Actually a marriage in which no quarreling at all takes place may well be one that is dead or dying from emotional undernourishment. If you care, you probably fight.

—British author and composer FLORA DAVIS. Sometimes war between the sexes—or at least a minor skirmish—can actually be salubrious.

Why does a woman work ten years to change a man's habits and then complain that he's not the man she married?

—Singer BARBRA STREISAND. (Only ten years? We should be so lucky . . .)

Sexiness wears thin after a while and beauty fades, but to be married to a man who makes you laugh every day, ah, now that's a real treat!

—Actress JOANNE WOODWARD, the merry Mrs. of actor Paul Newman.

I cannot abide the Mr. and Mrs. Noah attitude towards marriage; the animals went in two by two, forever stuck together with glue.

—Creative writer VITA SACKVILLE-WEST, who evaded the stultifying two-plus-two scenario by marrying a gay man, and romancing her female friends.

So many persons who think divorce is a panacea for every ill find out, when they try it, that the remedy is worse than the disease.

    —Turn-of-the-century sob sister DOROTHY DIX (aka Elizabeth Gilmer), reluctant to declare a marriage moribund unless one of the parties had stopped breathing.

Love is much nicer to be in than an automobile accident, a tight girdle, a higher tax bracket, or a holding pattern over Philadelphia.

    —Poet JUDITH VIORST, looking on the positive side of twentieth-century passion.

$\mathcal{Y}$ou need someone to love you while you're looking for someone to love.

—Writer SHELAGH DELANEY, a devout believer in romantic duplicity.

$\mathcal{I}$f you want to say it with flowers, remember that a single rose screams in your face: "I'm cheap!"

—"Designing Woman" DELTA BURKE, a babe who believes in abundance.

I think, therefore I'm single.

*W*hen my mom found my diaphragm, I told her it was a bathing cap for my cat.

I rely on my personality for birth control.

—Bachelorette LIZ WINSTON, who won't be hitting you up for a layette set anytime soon.

My marriage didn't work out. I was a human being and he was a Klingon.

    —CAROL LIEFER. By comparison, being mated to a Martian is probably a piece of cake.

$What$ ever happened to the kind of love leech that lived in his car and dropped by once a month to throw up and use you for your shower? Now all these pigs want is a *commitment*.

    —Comedian JUDY TENUTA, the disgruntled, self-designated "Goddess of Love."

Prolix

Professionals

$\mathcal{W}$hat I wanted to be when I grew up was—in charge.

—WILMA VAUGHT, Brigadier General of the U.S. Air Force.

$\mathcal{G}$ive me my sword.

—OVETA HOBBY, first director of the Women's Army Corps, and a colonel nobody wanted to cross.

$\mathcal{T}$he only jobs for which no man is qualified are human incubators and wet nurse. Likewise, the only job for which no woman is or can be qualified is sperm donor.

—WILMA SCOTT HEIDE, R.N., enumerating the three textbook cases in which anatomy is indeed destiny.

$\mathcal{I}$ could have succeeded much easier in my career had I been a man.

—Financier HENRIETTA GREEN. Her anatomy notwithstanding, "The Witch of Wall Street" managed to invest her inheritance so shrewdly that she was acknowledged, at the turn of the century, as the wealthiest woman in the world.

*B*eing a performer was always my destiny. When I was born, the doctors didn't have to pop me to get me going. It was like, "Thank you, thank you. I am here!" I was ready to party.

—Comedic actress WHOOPI GOLDBERG. She had *joie de vivre* from Day One.

*B*roadway has been very good to me—but then I've been very good to Broadway.

—ETHEL MERMAN. During 1,147 performances of *Annie Get Your Gun,* the sharp-shooting showgirl managed to make her mark.

$\mathcal{I}$'m not surprised at what I've done.

—MARGARET KNIGHT, nineteenth-century inventor who patented more than two dozen types of heavy machinery.

$\mathcal{M}$y family wasn't the Brady Bunch. They were the Broody Bunch.

$\mathcal{M}$y father was a proctologist, my mother an abstract artist. That's how I see the world.

—SANDRA BERNHARD, a magnificently maladjusted entertainer.

One day I found myself saying to myself, "I can't live where I want to. I can't even say what I want to!" I decided I was a very stupid fool not to at least paint as I wanted to.

I don't much enjoy looking at paintings in general. I know too much about them. I take them apart.

—GEORGIA O'KEEFFE, doyenne of the painted desert. Convent-educated O'Keeffe also didn't enjoy hearing about the sexual symbolism of her work, insisting that any putative crotch imagery was nothing but a crock.

A photograph is a secret about a secret. The more it tells you the less you know.

I really believe there are things nobody would see if I didn't photograph them.

My favorite thing is to go where I've never been.

—Photographer DIANE ARBUS, whose penchant for peculiar-looking posers led her down some rather unusual paths.

*Y*ou come to doing what you do by not being able to do something.

—GRACE PALEY, failed poet, acclaimed short story writer.

I was thirty-seven, too old for a paper route, too young for social security, and too tired for an affair.

—ERMA BOMBECK, on her transformation from housewife into humorist.

$\mathcal{I}$ never thought I would fall on my face.

     —California-cuisine queen ALICE WATERS. And the souffle also rises.

$\mathcal{D}$ear, never forget one little point: It's my business. You just work here.

     —ELIZABETH ARDEN. The queen bee of her own cosmetics empire, arrogant Arden refused to issue stock to her business manager/spouse.

$\mathcal{T}$o love what you do and feel that it matters—how could anything be more fun?

—KATHARINE GRAHAM, extremely entertained publisher of the *Washington Post*.

$\mathcal{T}$he important thing in acting is to be able to laugh and cry. If I have to cry, I think of my sex life. If I have to laugh, I think of my sex life.

—GLENDA JACKSON, actress-turned-politician. As to what Glenda does when she has to act bored, we can only guess.

Oh, I suppose it's some kind of an affliction.

—GINGER ROGERS, Fred Astaire's favorite partner, on her determination to be a dancer.

I studied men and adapted myself to their world. I tried to emulate them. Eventually, I realized that I didn't have to "become" a man to be powerful.

—Choreographer TWYLA THARP, no longer bending over backward to be one of the guys.

This is the oppressor's language.

—ADRIENNE RICH, articulating her primary problem as a radical feminist poet.

Every actor has a natural animosity toward every other actor, present or absent, living or dead.

—LOUISE BROOKS, actress. In her profession, everyone wanted to be the prima donna.

$\mathcal{W}$e cannot take anything for granted, beyond the first mathematical formulae. Question everything else.

—MARIA MITCHELL, astronomer. As a Vassar professor, she especially encouraged her students to question the superiority of men in scientific affairs.

$\mathcal{T}$he glass ceiling gets more pliable when you turn up the heat!

—PAULINE R. KEZER, Connecticut Secretary of State, plotting a patriarchal melt-down.

I shall be an autocrat; that's my trade. And the good Lord will forgive me; that's His.

*Y*ou philosophers are lucky men. You write on paper, and paper is patient. Unfortunate Empress that I am, I write on the susceptible skins of living beings.

—CATHERINE **II**, Empress of Russia, bitching about her job.

$\mathcal{E}$verywhere I go, I'm asked if I think the universities stifle writers. My opinion is that they don't stifle enough of them. There's many a best seller that could have been prevented by a good teacher.

—Fiction-writer FLANNERY O'CONNOR, not the nurturing type.

$\mathcal{A}$ll books are either dreams or swords. You can cut or you can drug with words.

—AMY LOWELL, enormously eccentric poet, on the versatility of prose.

$\mathcal{E}$.M. Forster never gets any further than warming the teapot. He's a rare fine hand at that. Feel this teapot. Is it not beautifully warm? Yes, but there ain't going to be no tea.

—Short-story writer KATHERINE MANSFIELD. In her line of work, it was essential to advance the plot, not admire the pot.

$\mathcal{I}$f I didn't start painting, I would have raised chickens.

—GRANDMA MOSES, a very pragmatic primitivist.

Men,
Schmen

$\mathcal{T}$his book is dedicated to all those men who betrayed me at one time or another, in hopes they will fall off their motorcycles and break their necks.

    —Poet DIANE WAKOSKI, graciously acknowledging the male muses who inspired her *Motorcycle Betrayal Poems*.

$\mathcal{I}$ don't have buried anger against men. Because my anger is right on the surface.

$\mathcal{T}$here is no female Mozart because there is no female Jack the Ripper.

$\mathcal{M}$ichaelangelo was a pornographer.

    —CAMILLE PAGLIA. As a child, the provocative Ph.D. hinted at her sexual persona-to-be by celebrating Halloween costumed as Napoleon, a Roman soldier, and the toreador from *Carmen*.

When a man gives his opinion he's a man. When a woman gives her opinion she's a bitch.

I have always been driven by some distant music—a battle hymn no doubt—for I have been at war from the beginning. I've never looked back before. I've never had the time, and it has always seemed so dangerous. To look back is to relax one's vigil.

I am a woman meant for a man, but I never found a man who could compete.

—BETTE DAVIS. Off-screen, the star of *All About Eve* had a hard time scaring up a satisfactory Adam.

If men can run the world, why can't they stop wearing neckties? How intelligent is it to start the day by tying a little noose around your neck?

—LINDA ELLERBEE, broadcast journalist. Since her 1989 stint at the Betty Ford Clinic, the former darling of five networks has discontinued her own policy of tying one on daily. And so it goes.

If it's so natural to kill, why do men have to go into training to learn how?

—JOAN BAEZ, the world's most persistent peacenik.

*I*t's a man's world, and you men can have it.

—KATHERINE ANNE PORTER. Though widely travelled, the anarchistic novelist still wasn't a citizen of the world.

*T*he only time a woman really succeeds in changing a man is when he's a baby.

—NATALIE WOOD, professional leading lady who failed to alter the behavior of beaux Elvis Presley, Warren Beatty, or Frank Sinatra.

*I*f boys are better, why should a male choose to love an inferior female? If a penis is so great, two penises should be even greater.

—LETTY COTTIN POGREBIN, author of numerous feminist tomes, including *How To Make It In a Man's World* (first of all, it seems, it helps to be a man).

$\mathcal{B}$eing a sex symbol was rather like being a convict.

$\mathcal{T}$here aren't any hard women, only soft men.

—RAQUEL WELCH, notorious both for her annoyingly firm form and for her role as one-half of a transsexual character in the 1970 film *Myra Breckenridge*.

I wonder why men can get serious at all. They have this delicate long thing hanging outside their bodies, which goes up and down by its own will . . . If I were a man I would always be laughing at myself.

—YOKO ONO, mature multi-media artist also amused by the derrière (her 1967 film *Bottoms*, for example, featured 365 bare posteriors).

$\mathcal{A}$ll men are rapists and that's all they are. They rape us with their eyes, their laws, and their codes.

—MARILYN FRENCH, who plotted her counter-attack against the chauvinist conspiracy in *The Women's Room*.

$\mathcal{I}$ got it. I grabbed it by my right hand. And when I grabbed it, I gave it a yank. And when I yanked it, I twisted all at the same time.

—CURTESCINE LLOYD, middle-aged Mississippian who refused to cooperate with a would-be rapist. Instead, Ms. Lloyd seized the assailant by the salient portion of his anatomy, squeezing insistently until he was incapable of committing the intended crime.

*T*here's nineteen men livin' in my neighborhood:
Eighteen of them are fools
and the one ain't no doggone good.

   —BESSIE SMITH. For the hard-living "Empress of the Blues," man trouble was her bread and butter.

*I*f you do it psychologically, it's so much more fun.

   —FLORENCE KING on Lorena Bobbitt. Also, it isn't a felony.

*M*en get their opinions as boys learn to spell,
By reiteration chiefly.

    —Poet ELIZABETH BARRETT BROWNING, more popular with
nineteenth-century readers than her beloved Bobby B.

*N*o one is more arrogant toward women, more aggressive or scornful,
than the man who is anxious about his virility.

    —SIMONE DE BEAUVOIR. To those who took *The Second Sex* seriously,
brainy de Beauvoir was Sartre's more significant Other.

I'm not denyin' that women are foolish; God Almighty made 'em to match the men.

*H*e was like a cock who thought the sun had risen to hear him crow.

—GEORGE ELIOT. The noted Victorian novelist adopted a male pen name, but kept her own point of view.

I have had my belly full of great men (forgive the expression). I quite like to read about them in the pages of Plutarch, where they don't outrage my humanity. Let us see them carved in marble or cast in bronze, and hear no more about them. In real life they are nasty creatures, persecutors, temperamental, despotic, bitter and suspicious.

—GEORGE SAND. Another nineteenth-century George who was really a gal, scandalous Sand was noted both for her reformist novels and her numerous extra-marital affairs.

$\mathcal{I}$ blame Rousseau, myself. "Man is born free," indeed. Man is not born free, he is born attached to his mother by a cord and is not capable of looking after himself for at least seven years (seventy in some cases).

—Journalist KATHARINE WHITEHORN, still waiting to celebrate Independence Day.

$\mathcal{A}$ man is two people, himself and his cock. A man always takes his friend to the party. Of the two, the friend is the nicer, being more able to show his feelings.

—Novelist BERYL BAINBRIDGE, who knows when a guy is glad to see her.

$\mathcal{T}$he difference between government bonds and men is that government bonds mature.

—DEBBIE PERRY, an informed investor.

$\mathcal{D}$on't accept rides from strange men, and remember that all men are strange.

—Writer ROBIN MORGAN, who in a more separatist phase maintained that the *Sisterhood Is Powerful* enough to get there on its own unshaven legs.

$\mathcal{W}$hatever women do they must do twice as well as men to be thought half as good. Luckily, this is not difficult.

—CHARLOTTE WHITTON, mathematically gifted mayor of Ottawa.

Give a man a fish and he eats for a day. Teach him how to fish and you get rid of him for the whole weekend.

—ZENNA SCHAFFER, happy to be off the hook.

Domestic Dissidents

$\mathcal{W}$henever I date a guy, I think, is this the man I want my children to spend their weekends with?

—Stand-up comic RITA RUDNER, a person who likes to look at the big picture.

*B*eing a mother is a noble status, right? Right. So why does it change when you put "unwed" or "welfare" in front of it?

*I*f men could get pregnant, abortion would be a sacrament.

—Civil rights lawyer FLORYNCE KENNEDY, once lionized by the press as "Radicalism's Rudest Mouth" and as a "loud-mouthed middle-aged colored lady" by herself.

A printed card means nothing except that you are too lazy to write to the woman who has done more for you than anyone in the world. And candy! You take a box to Mother—and then eat most of it yourself. A pretty sentiment.

—ANNA JARVIS, founder of Mother's Day. In the end, she squandered Mom's entire estate on a campaign to prevent the Hallmarking of the holiday.

$\mathcal{I}$'m hostile to the act of childbirth—I've always found the concept of childbirth to be a morbid one at best—something *nostalgic* that a West Coast "return to nature" cult would espouse.

—Controversial composer DIAMANDA GALAS, simultaneously slammed by forty Italian newspapers for using her voice as "a tool of torture and destruction."

$\mathcal{I}$'ve been married to one Marxist and one Fascist, and neither one would take the garbage out.

—Actress LEE GRANT. Sorry to say, she never tied the knot with a member of the compost-conscious Green Party.

$\mathcal{I}$n twenty years I've never had a day when I didn't have to think about someone else's needs. And this means the writing has to be fitted around it.

—ALICE MUNRO, child-bearing author.

$\mathcal{T}$here's a time when you have to explain to your children why they're born, and it's a marvelous thing if you know the reason by then.

—Jazz artist HAZEL SCOTT, whose divorce from Congressman Adam Clayton Powell followed close on the heels of her performance in *The Night Affair*.

$\mathcal{I}$ hate housework! You make the beds, you do the dishes—and six months later you have to start all over again.

—JOAN RIVERS, chatty talk show host who gets more mileage out of her bust than her dust-buster.

$\mathcal{I}$ am a marvelous housekeeper. Every time I leave a man I keep his house.

—ZSA ZSA GABOR, actress/property owner who, eight divorces notwithstanding, "has never hated a man enough to give him his diamonds back."

*H*ousework isn't bad in itself—the trouble with it is that it's inhumanely lonely.

—PAT LOUD, ex-homemaker who enjoyed the constant company of in-house camera crews during the filming of *An American Family,* PBS's twelve-episode documentary chronicling the collapse of her marriage.

I don't pretend to be an ordinary housewife.

I've been through it all, baby, I'm Mother Courage.

—The one and never-lonely ELIZABETH TAYLOR, temporarily wed to (among others) an ordinary construction worker.

I love children, especially when they cry, for then someone takes them away.

    —Novelist NANCY MITFORD. Books were her thing, not babies.

*Y*ou can't get spoiled if you do your own ironing.

    —Actress MERYL STREEP—starchy, but not self-indulgent.

The most effective form of birth control I know is spending the day with my kids.

—JILL BENSLEY, another pooped parent.

Babies don't need fathers, but mothers do. Someone who is taking care of a baby needs to be taken care of.

—AMY HECKERLING, conceptualizing a very co-dependent family.

$\mathcal{T}$he only thing that seems eternal and natural in motherhood is ambivalence.

 —JANE LAZARRE. Running away is a maternal instinct, too.

$\mathcal{W}$e want better reasons for having children than not knowing how to prevent them.

 —British feminist DORA RUSSELL. She didn't have to be the mother of Bertrand Russell's kids.

*G*iving birth is like taking your lower lip and forcing it over your head.

    —Comedian CAROL BURNETT, stretching it just a bit.

I was going to commit suicide by sticking my head in the oven, but there was a cake in it.

    —LESLIE BOONE, too busy to self-destruct.

Peeved
Eves

The militant, not the meek, shall inherit the earth.

I am not afraid of the pen, or the scaffold, or the sword. I will tell the truth wherever I please.

Pray for the dead and fight like hell for the living.

    —MOTHER JONES. This mother was a woman of powerful passions.

A woman that's too soft and sweet is like tapioca pudding—fine for them as likes it.

—OSA JOHNSON, jungle explorer who could cope with cobras, but not "the dangers of civilization."

*I*t's time to stop denying the "inner bitch" in ourselves. Stop apologizing for her. Set her free.

—*Hysteria* magazine contributor ELIZABETH HILTS. And the hell with the inner child too!

*O*f course I realized there was a measure of danger. Obviously I faced the possibility of not returning when first I considered going. Once faced and settled there really wasn't any good reason to refer to it.

—AMELIA EARHART, the first female aviator to soar successfully across the Atlantic, and the first to disappear without a trace while attempting to circumnavigate the globe.

Once I decide to do something, I can't have people telling me I can't. If there's a roadblock, you jump over it, walk around it, crawl under it.

—KITTY KELLEY, extremely limber (and, according to some, extremely imaginative) celebrity biographer.

Slaying the dragon of delay is no sport for the short-winded.

—SANDRA DAY O'CONNOR, aerobically accomplished Supreme Court Justice.

Girlhood . . . is the intellectual phase of a woman's life, that time when, unencumbered by societal expectations or hormonal rages, one may pursue any curiosity from the mysteries of a yo-yo to the meaning of infinity. These two particular pursuits were where I left off in the fifth grade when I discovered a hair growing in the wrong place and all hell broke loose.

—Essayist and ex-nurse ALICE KAHN. *Sans* those secondary sex characteristics, she might have been the next Albert Einstein.

$\mathcal{W}$hen people keep telling you that you can't do a thing, you kind of like to try it.

—MARGARET CHASE SMITH, Maine politician who tried four terms in the U.S. House of Representatives and another four in the Senate.

$\mathcal{L}$ife is either always a tight-rope or a feather bed. Give me the tight-rope.

—EDITH WHARTON, stiff-spined Pulitzer Prize winner who deplored the vulgarity of post-Victorian America.

$\mathcal{I}$ cannot and will not cut my conscience to fit this year's fashions.

$\mathcal{I}$ like people who refuse to speak until they are ready to speak.

$\mathcal{C}$ynicism is an unpleasant way of saying the truth.

—Playwright LILLIAN HELLMAN, who declined an invitation to chat
with the House Un-American Activities Committee in 1952.

$\mathcal{N}$obody can make you feel inferior without your consent.

$\mathcal{I}$t's better to light a candle than to curse the darkness.

$\mathcal{Y}$ou must do the thing you think you cannot do.

—ELEANOR ROOSEVELT. Her globe-trotting campaigns for good causes (and not her extra-marital mash on journalist Lorena Hickock) earned America's most admired First Lady the nickname of "Eleanor Everywhere."

"We, the people of the United States." Which "We, the people"? The women were not included.

—Suffragist LUCY STONE. She took her semantics seriously, but not her husband's last name.

There is no female mind. The brain is not an organ of sex. Might as well speak of a female liver.

—CHARLOTTE PERKINS GILMAN, nineteenth-century activist who titled her autobiography *The Living* [and not, one notes, *The Liver*] *of Charlotte Perkins Gilman*.

*B*ut oh, what a woman I should be if an able young man would consecrate his life to me as secretaries and technicians do to their men employers.

　　—MABEL ULRICH, early twentieth-century physician. (A wife would also have been nice.)

*I*f women can sleep their way to the top, how come they aren't there? . . . There must be an epidemic of insomnia out there.

　　—ELLEN GOODMAN, skeptical syndicated columnist.

[Women] are early taught that to appear to yield, is the only way to govern.

I ask no favors for my sex . . . All I ask of our brethren is that they will take their feet from off our necks.

—SARAH MOORE GRIMKÉ, one of the first abolitionists to link the oppression of women with the oppression of slaves. (Ms. Grimké was not, however, the first individual to find patriarchal society a major pain in the neck.)

I do not believe in sex distinction in literature, law, politics, or trade—or that modesty and virtue are more becoming to women than to men, but wish we had more of it everywhere.

—BELVA LOCKWOOD, 1884 presidential candidate who definitely did not have a Gary Hart problem. (Also, she definitely did not win the election.)

I asked for bread, and got a stone in the shape of a pedestal.

Women have been called queens for a long time, but the kingdom given them isn't worth ruling.

—LOUISA MAY ALCOTT, a fierce feminist who resented her publisher's suggestion to write about *Little Women*—but not the resulting royalties.

$\mathcal{T}$o assess the damage is a dangerous act.

—Playwright CHERRIÉ MORAGA, radical writer for a brave new world.

$\mathcal{O}$f all the nasty outcomes predicted for a women's liberation . . . none was more alarming, from a feminist point of view, than the suggestion that women would eventually become just like men.

—Journalist BARBARA EHRENREICH. As if.

*I*t was we, the people; not we, the white male citizens; nor yet we, the male citizens; but we, the whole people, who formed the union.

*M*en, their rights and nothing more;
women, their rights and nothing less.

*C*autious, careful people, always casting about to preserve their reputations . . . can never effect a reform.

—Silver-dollar suffragist SUSAN B. ANTHONY, the power behind the nineteenth-century push for equal rights.

$\mathcal{T}$he king has been very good to me. He promoted me from a simple maid to be a . . . queen. Now he will raise me to be a martyr.

—ANNE BOLEYN, second spouse of Henry VIII. Though horrid Henry sentenced her to death for failing to produce a male heir, Queen Anne managed not to badmouth him on en route to her beheading. Well, not overtly, anyway.

$\mathcal{I}$ resent the idea that people would blame the messenger for the message, rather than looking at the content of the message itself.

—ANITA HILL, the woman who helped America learn how to spell harassment.

$\mathcal{W}$omen are the true maintenance class. Society is built upon their acquiescence, and upon their small and necessary labors.

$\mathcal{I}$ became a feminist as an alternative to becoming a masochist.

—Journalist SALLY KEMPTON, a long-suffering social critic.

*N*o zoologist, as far as I know, has ever observed that animals rape in their natural habitat, the wild.

*W*e are unalterably opposed to the presentation of the female body being stripped, bound, raped, tortured, mutilated, and murdered in the name of commercial entertainment and free speech.

—Strident feminist SUSAN BROWNMILLER, still trying to take all the fun out of being a guy.

$\mathcal{W}$e haven't come a long way, we've come a short way. If we hadn't come a short way, no one would be calling us "baby".

—Social critic ELIZABETH JANEWAY—smoldering, but not actually smoking..

$\mathcal{T}$he vote means nothing to women. We should be armed.

—Embittered novelist EDNA O'BRIEN, one of Ireland's finest exports.

Racy Remarks

You can be up to your boobies in white satin, with gardenias in your hair and no sugar cane for miles, but you can still be working on a plantation.

You've got to have something to eat and a little love in your life before you can hold still for any damn body's sermon on how to behave.

   —BILLIE HOLIDAY, who sang like an angel, and saw more than her share of hell.

$\mathcal{I}$ do not weep at the world—I am too busy sharpening my oyster knife.

$\mathcal{S}$ometimes, I feel discriminated against, but it does not make me angry. It merely astonishes me. How *can* any deny themselves the pleasure of my company? It's beyond me.

—ZORA NEALE HURSTON, Barnard-educated belle-lettrist of the Harlem Renaissance.

$\mathcal{W}$hen I am alone I am not aware of my race or my sex, both in need of social contexts for definition.

—MAXINE HONG KINGSTON, not a woman warrior in private.

$\mathcal{T}$here is nowhere you can go and only be with people who are like you. Give it up.

—Cultural historian and founder of Sweet Honey in the Rock, BERNICE JOHNSON REAGON. Ms. Reagon's various hangouts have included the curator's office at the National Museum of History, the stage of Carnegie Hall, and a jail cell following a student protest march.

Sometimes, it's like a hair across your cheek. You can't see it, you can't find it with your fingers, but you keep brushing at it because the feel of it is irritating.

I could not run away from the situation. I had become, whether I liked it or not, a symbol, representing my people. I had to appear.

—MARIAN ANDERSON, on racism. Though the acclaimed singer debuted at the Metropolitan Opera, the Daughters of the American Revolution insisted she just wouldn't blend in with the color scheme at Constitution Hall.

$\mathcal{M}$y literary agenda begins by acknowledging that America has transformed *me*. It does not end until I show how I (and the hundreds of thousands like me) have transformed America.

—BHARATI MUKHERJEE, the first naturalized American citizen to win the National Book Critics Circle Award.

$\mathcal{I}$f they come for me in the morning, they will come for you at night.

—African-American activist ANGELA DAVIS. Formerly a fugitive on the FBI's "ten mostwanted" list, now in great demand as a lecturer at institutions of higher education.

$\mathcal{I}$ speak to the black experience, but I am always talking about the human condition—about what we can endure, dream, fail at, and still survive.

—Writer MAYA ANGELOU, whose fate was foretold, sort of, by Billie Holliday: "You're going to be famous but it won't be for singing." Still, music played its part in multi-talented Maya's renown: most Americans recall her primarily as the author of the best-selling autobiographical novel *I Know Why The Caged Bird Sings*.

$\mathscr{I}$t is the mind that makes the body.

$\mathscr{W}$e do as much, we eat as much, we want as much.

    —Ex-slave and suffragist SOJOURNER TRUTH. Her name said it all.

$\mathcal{I}$ found, while thinking about the far-reaching world of the creative black woman, that often the truest answer to a question that really matters can be found very close.

—ALICE WALKER, who called the concerns of black women to the attention of Americans of every hue in her Pulitzer Prize-winning novel, *The Color Purple*.

I no more thought of style or literary excellence than the mother who rushes into the street and cries for help to save her children from a burning house, thinks of the teachings of the rhetorician or the elocutionist.

—HARRIET BEECHER STOWE, on writing *Uncle Tom's Cabin*. For better or worse, the novel that some say caused the Civil War came from the heart, not from the head.

*I*n my early days I was a sepia-colored Hedy Lamarr. Now I'm black and a woman, singing my own way.

    —Singer LENA HORNE, no longer white-washed for cross-cultural consumption.

*T*he one thing that doesn't abide by majority rule is a person's conscience.

    —HARPER LEE. The vast majority of readers agreed that Lee's bestselling anti-racist novel, *To Kill a Mockingbird,* was a stunning *tour de force*.

$\mathscr{M}$y only concern was to get home after a hard day's work.

—ROSA PARKS, the tired tailor's assistant who stood up for her rights—and sparked the Civil Rights movement of the 1950s—by refusing to give up her seat on a segregated bus.

$\mathscr{I}$ started with this idea in my head, "There's two things I've got a right to, death or liberty."

—HARRIET TUBMAN, conductor-in-chief of the Underground Railway.

$\mathcal{I}$ haven't seen anyone killed, and I have yet to kill anyone. I have exhibited *great restraint!*

—Former *Days of Our Life* staffer WANDA COLEMAN, who now prefers to write about black pride and prejudice instead of amnesia and adultery.

Aged Sages

In our family we don't divorce our men—we bury them.

To be somebody you must last.

—RUTH GORDON, whose *tour de force* as the septuagenarian seductress in *Harold and Maude* was a major turn-on for swinging audiences in the seventies.

*A*ge is something that doesn't matter, unless you are a cheese.

—BILLIE BURKE, aka Mrs. Flo Ziegfeld, cast as one of *The Young Philadelphians* at the ripe old age of seventy-four.

I'll be eighty this month. Age, if nothing else, entitles me to set the record straight before I dissolve. I've given my memoirs far more thought than any of my marriages. You can't divorce a book.

—Silent screen superstar GLORIA SWANSON. In earlier days, she was the soul of discretion about her dalliance with Joseph P. Kennedy.

$\mathcal{T}$he reason some men fear older women is they fear their own mortality.

$\mathcal{I}$ believe the second half of one's life is meant to be better than the first half. The first half is finding out how you do it. And the second half is enjoying it.

—FRANCES LEAR, founder/editor of *Lear's*, the nation's only mass-circulation magazine for women too mature to have any genuine interest in advertisements for pimple cream.

$\mathcal{I}$'m usually out Monday through Thursday nights. I've been going like this for years. Without a husband, it's a lot easier. No husband wants to go out every night.

$\mathcal{W}$hen I was 40, I used to wonder what people thought of me. Now I wonder what *I* think of them.

—Socialite BROOKE ASTOR at 92—still curious, but no longer self-conscious.

*W*isdom doesn't automatically come with old age. Nothing does—except wrinkles. It's true, some wines improve with age. But only if the grapes were good in the first place.

—ABIGAIL VAN BUREN, professional student of human nature, amateur viticulturist.

I have bursts of being a lady, but it doesn't last long.

*N*ow that I'm over sixty, I'm veering toward respectability.

    —Well-seasoned sexpert SHELLY WINTERS, still making the rounds on the titillating talk-show circuit.

*T*here are three things I've yet to do: Opera, rodeo and porno.

—Actress BEA ARTHUR at the age of 67, shortly before doing the diva thing (in a non-singing role) with the Metropolitan Opera. Next on the agenda: "Maude Does Minneapolis"?

*Y*ou cannot just waste time. Otherwise you'll die to regret it.

—HARRIET DOERR, who received her B.A. at the age of sixty-seven and published her first novel at seventy-four.

I have everything I had twenty years ago, only it's all a little bit lower.

  —Striptease artist GYPSY ROSE LEE, pondering the ephemeral nature of perkiness.

*T*he secret of staying young is to live honestly, eat slowly, and lie about your age.

  —LUCILLE BALL, the loopy *Lucy* that America loved.

$\mathcal{P}$reparing for the worst is an activity I have taken up since I turned thirty-five, and the worst actually began to happen.

—Humorist DELIA EPHRON, a pessimist who plans ahead.

$\mathcal{T}$he lovely thing about being forty is that you can appreciate twenty-five-year-old men more.

—COLLEEN MCCULLOUGH, Australian neurophysiologist-turned-novelist. Now, if only being forty also made twenty-five-year-old men appreciate *you* more . . .

$\mathcal{F}$rom birth to age 18, a girl needs good parents, from 18 to 35 she needs good looks, from 35 to 55 she needs a good personality, and from 55 on she needs cash.

—Vaudevillian SOPHIE TUCKER. An entertainer to the end of her days, "The Last of the Red-Hot Mamas" spent nearly thirty years in the "Needs Cash" category.

$\mathcal{T}$he hardest years in life are those between ten and seventy.

—HELEN HAYES, the legendary (and long-lived) actress, at the age of eighty-three.

$\mathcal{A}$n archaeologist is the best husband a woman can have; the older she gets, the more interested he is in her.

—Author AGATHA CHRISTIE, on how to preserve one's maidenly mystery forever.

$\mathcal{T}$his is a youth-oriented society, and the joke is on them because youth is a disease from which we all recover.

—DOROTHY FULDHEIM, on the pathology of being in one's prime.

The ultimate indignity is to be given a bedpan by a stranger who calls you by your first name.

I enjoy my wrinkles and regard them as badges of distinction—I've worked hard for them!

—MAGGIE KUHN. The founder of the Gray Panthers wasn't fond of being treated like a child.

The great thing about getting older is that you don't lose all the other ages you've been . . .

    —MADELEINE L'ENGLE. The woman who wrote a *Wrinkle in Time* might misplace her house keys, but her memories remained intact.

Quite a few women told me, one way or another, that they thought it was sex, not youth, that's wasted on the young.

    —Researcher JANET HARRIS. This just in: Adults enjoy sex!

I'm at an age where my back goes out more than I do.

*T*hink of me as a sex symbol for the men who don't give a damn.

   —Comedian PHYLLIS DILLER. At the age of seventy-three, Ms. Diller posed as a poster girl for San Francisco's public transportation system, thereby also becoming a symbol for commuters who didn't give a damn if they showed up for work on time.

Phallus-Free Philosophy

Reality is something you rise above.

—LIZA MINNELLI, perpetually plagued by her problematic "z."

*S*in brought death, and death will disappear with the disappearance of sin.

*M*atter and death are mortal illusions.

—MARY BAKER EDDY, the deceased founder of the Church of Christian Science.

I don't want life to imitate art. I want life to be art.

*I*nstant gratification takes too long.

—CARRIE FISHER, a major film star at the age of twenty-one.

$\mathcal{I}$t is not true that life is one damn thing after another—it's one damn thing over and over.

$\mathcal{I}$ love humanity but I hate people.

—Perturbed poet EDNA ST. VINCENT MILLAY. (Burning the candle at both ends, it seems, doesn't really bring out the best in *anyone*.)

The most popular labor-saving device is still money.

—PHYLLIS GEORGE, sportscaster by trade, multi-millionaire by marriage.

Only the little people pay taxes.

—Hotel magnate LEONA HELMSLEY, who subsequently did time in the big house for tax evasion.

Smoking kills. If you're killed, you've lost a very important part of your life.

—Actress BROOKE SHIELDS, Princeton graduate.

Expiring for love is beautiful but stupid.

Lack of charisma can be fatal.

—JENNY HOLZER, internationally acclaimed artist who actually earns a living inventing new clichés.

*N*ever face facts; if you do you'll never get up in the morning.

—MARLO THOMAS, *That Girl* who played the role of TV's first independent career woman, only to wind up as the real-life wife of Phil Donahue.

*S*cience may have found a cure for most evils; but it has found no remedy for the worst of them all—the apathy of human beings.

*T*he heresy of one age becomes the orthodoxy of the next.

    —Blind visionary HELEN KELLER, who saw some things more clearly than others.

$\mathcal{T}$here must be quite a few things a hot bath won't cure, but I don't know many of them.

—SYLVIA PLATH, author of *The Bell Jar*. Her ultimate solution for psychic stress wasn't nearly as copasetic.

$\mathcal{I}$f women ruled the world and we all got massages, there would be no war.

$\mathcal{N}$o day is so bad it can't be fixed with a nap.

    —CARRIE SNOW, stand-up comic who would really like to lie down for a while.

*M*oney has nothing to do with style at all, but naturally it helps every situation.

—Fashion editor DIANA VREELAND. Big bucks keep the "Beautiful People" (a phrase coined by the voguish Ms. V.) from feeling blah.

*T*he art of being a woman can never consist of being a bad imitation of a man.

—OLGA KNOPF, psychiatrist. Sometimes a cigar is just a cigar, but it's never a Virginia Slim.

*N*either birth nor sex forms a limit to genius.

    —CHARLOTTE BRONTË, god-like Gothic novelist. To err is human; to write *Jane Eyre* was divine.

*C*reative minds have always been known to survive any kind of bad training.

    —Psychoanalyst ANNA FREUD, who survived Papa Sigmund by several decades.

One never notices what has been done; one can only see what remains to be done.

—MARIE CURIE. Was the Type A physicist too busy to take note of her two Nobel Prizes?

I have always had a dread of becoming a passenger in life.

—QUEEN MARGRETHE II of Denmark, a country with a diminished demand for chauffeurs.

I've always been independent, and I don't see how it conflicts with femininity.

    —Economist SYLVIA PORTER. Needless to say, the supposed dichotomy that puzzles Ms. Porter has been a mystery to women throughout history.

*T*his life isn't bad for a first draft.

    —Journalist JOAN KONNER. On the other hand, the ending seems a little abrupt . . .

$\mathcal{N}$o matter how big or soft or warm your bed is, you still have to get out of it.

    —GRACE SLICK, raucous rock diva of Jefferson Airplane fame (and vintage).

$\mathcal{T}$he only thing that makes life possible is permanent, intolerable uncertainty; not knowing what comes next.

    —Science fiction writer URSULA K. LE GUIN, one of the first female scribes to venture where no woman had gone before.

$\mathcal{W}$hy not seize the pleasure at once? How often is happiness destroyed by preparation, foolish preparation!

$\mathcal{I}$ do not want people to be agreeable, as it saves me the trouble of liking them.

—Nineteenth-century novelist JANE AUSTEN, prejudiced against the perky, and proud of it.

*B*eing popular is important. Otherwise people might not like you.

 —Humorist MIMI POND, putting her finger (and never mind which one) squarely on the number one concern of most American high school students.

I think it's one of the scars in our culture that we have too high an opinion of ourselves. We align ourselves with the angels instead of the higher primates.

 —ANGELA CARTER, British educator. Think chimps, not champs.

A perfectly normal person is rare in our civilization.

—Psychoanalyst KAREN HORNEY. Under her unshrinking scrutiny, the concept of penis envy shriveled up and rolled into a harmless little ball.

*N*ot only is life a bitch, it has puppies.

*L*iving in a vacuum sucks.

I have often relied on the blindness of strangers.

    —ADRIENNE E. GUSOFF, goofing on the zany late 20th-century zeitgeist.

$\mathcal{A}$lcoholism, crime, insanity, suicide, divorce, drug addiction and even impotency are often merely the results of bad eating.

    —Nutritionist ADELLE DAVIS. Unfortunately, Davis' ultimate impact on the American diet was somewhat diminished by an unfortunate preoccupation with brewer's yeast and the fact that she was not, in the end, Julia Child.

$\mathcal{L}$ife itself is the proper binge.

     —Chef JULIA CHILD, top name in TV dinners.

$\mathcal{I}$ moved to New York City for my health. I'm paranoid and it was the only place where my fears were justified.

     —ANITA WEISS. A bite of the Big Apple each day keeps the psychiatrist away.

$\mathcal{T}$he trouble with the rat race is that even if you win, you're still a rat.

$\mathcal{W}$hen we talk to God, we're praying. When God talks to us, we're schizophrenic.

$\mathcal{J}$ust remember, we're all in this alone.

    —LILY TOMLIN, one of the few sure signs of intelligent life in the universe.

Index

T